LOOKING BEYOND
BREXIT

Graham Tomlin is Bishop of Kensington.

LOOKING BEYOND BREXIT

Bringing the country back together

Graham Tomlin

First published in Great Britain in 2019

Society for Promoting Christian Knowledge
36 Causton Street
London SW1P 4ST
www.spck.org.uk

British Library Cataloguing-in-Publication Data
A catalogue record for this book is available from the British Library

ISBN 978 0 281 08427 2
eBook ISBN 978 0 281 08428 9

Typeset by The Book Guild Ltd, Leicester, UK

First printed in Great Britain by Ashford Colour Press

Subsequently digitally reprinted in Great Britain

eBook by The Book Guild Ltd, Leicester, UK

To all my friends who voted
either Leave or Remain

Contents

'Britain goes it alone'

It's a headline that could have been written nearly 500 years ago. For this is not the first time Britain has proposed breaking away from a big pan-European project, seeking to build a new set of relationships around the world while experiencing deep divisions at home. Over the past three years, many have spotted echoes between Brexit and the English Reformation. In 1533, after much debate within the nation over its relationship with the European-wide Catholic Church – which had been flexing its muscles and expanding its claims to power – Henry VIII decided on a different kind of Brexit. Desiring an annulment of his marriage, and taking advantage of religious and political turmoil, he agreed to the English Church declaring independence, not this time from Brussels, but from Rome. The 1534 Act of Supremacy – a sixteenth-century version of Article 50 – recognized the

Monarch as Supreme Head of the Church in England rather than the Pope.

Some on the 'Leave' side of the Brexit debate, such as Ian Duncan Smith and Giles Fraser, have argued that the Reformation was an example of Britain releasing itself from the domination of an overblown, dictatorial European institution that had become top-heavy and too ambitious in its claim for control. Historians on the 'Remain' side, such as Diarmaid MacCulloch and Simon Sharma, have disputed this reading of events, pointing out that the Reformation was not a national independence movement, but was every bit as pan-European as the Roman Church. Indeed, Reform-minded churchmen kept up a remarkable correspondence and maintained communication across the Continent.

What has less often been remarked on is the long and difficult task of bringing a divided society together *after* the split from Rome. 1534 was not the end of the process of creating a new Britain; it was the beginning. Similarly, Brexit would by no means be the end of the process of our departure from the EU (despite all the talk of 'let's get Brexit done' and 'a clean break'). The English Church's declaration of independence was deeply contentious. Some, welcoming freedom from the 'tyranny of Rome', saw it as an opportunity for the nation to forge a new path in the world, with the glories of Elizabethan literature, the flowering of the English language and the growth of the British Empire yet to come. Others deplored it as a betrayal of solidarity with our continental neighbours and the Church that held Europe together, and foresaw disasters ahead.[1]

The immediate impact of the separation in England was traumatic. The nation lurched from Henry's ambivalence (despite manoeuvring to secure an annulment of his marriage, he was conservative when it came to church change), to the brief reign of his young son Edward VI (with a Privy Council that tried to push through Protestant reforms), to Mary Tudor's reign (which briefly attempted to bring England back under European papal control). Arguments raged and divisions ran deep. Truth was one of the casualties as lies were told to secure convictions; rumours spread to create scapegoats. The Pilgrimage of Grace, for example, a regional revolt of Yorkshire 'commoners', was fuelled by fear that local feudal rights were being overridden by a centralized government. People were also alarmed by unfounded reports that, as part of the religious changes, Henry was about to impose taxes on baptisms and confiscate all silver vessels, replacing them with tin. Thomas Cromwell's visitors routinely exaggerated the vices and extravagance of the English monasteries to justify Henry's policy of dissolution and the appropriation of resources for the crown. Fake news is nothing new.

Memorials in towns and cities throughout the country, and across the rest of Europe, still bear witness to this harrowing time, marking the sites of the ceremonial burning of martyrs for one cause or the other. Many had to emigrate for fear of persecution, and families were riven with conflict. In England, the path led through a civil war, whose causes were complex yet undeniably connected with some of the divisions laid bare by the Reformation a century earlier.

Nonetheless, an attempt was being made to find an alternative path.

A British solution

As a result of the Reformation, most nations and regions on the Continent tended to become either Protestant or Catholic, under the principle *cuius regio, eius religio* – which effectively meant that a ruler dictated the religion of those they ruled. In England, however, as Elizabeth I ascended the throne in 1558, constructive efforts were made to bring healing to a divided nation by combining the Catholic and Protestant strands of sixteenth-century religion within one national Church.

At the heart of the Reformation was a tussle between the local and the universal. Was Britain better off with an independent church under the authority of the monarch? Or tied into the broader, international Roman Church with links across western Europe? Would the Church of England thrive better as a loose collection of essentially independent local churches, or held together nationally under the authority of bishops and the crown?

There were diverse views in different parts of the country, even in neighbouring towns and villages. The Church of England that emerged was independent of Rome. It was rooted locally through the parish system inherited from the distant past. The relative independence of parishes – small geographical units under local leadership – enabled churches to embrace different styles, some more Catholic, some more Protestant, and adapt to neighbourhood sensitivities. Yet they were held together nationally through a commitment to creeds, a common form of worship, and allegiance to bishops and the Monarch, who was both head of state and head of the Church.

The Protestant, non-conformist Church that grew out of what is sometimes called the left wing of the Reformation put its emphasis on the importance of the local. Each individual church was independent, and there was little co-ordination or cohesion between one and another. The Roman Church, on the other hand, had a strong centre in Rome and with pope, cardinals and bishops in charge, was resistant to too much local improvisation. The emerging Church of England tried to hold together the local and the national, the Protestant and the Catholic. There was no attempt to blend them, to make a composite of the two that would blur their identities, but rather a search for unity that would embrace both, allow space for each perspective and expression, and yet hold to a set of common values, hard though that might be (it's not much easier now!)

Not everyone could buy into this. Catholics who were determined to stay under the Pope could not acquiesce to a church ruled by a monarch (especially a woman!), while Protestants could not accept the retaining of some ceremonial and structural parts of the medieval Catholic Church. Yet the Elizabethan Settlement – the religious and political arrangements made for England during the reign of Elizabeth I – tried to hold together convictions that in many places in Europe drove people apart. Christians were encouraged to recognize that what connected them across the church divides was stronger than what separated them. Despite the real differences, they could unite under a common structure, creeds and forms of worship, and the effort, however costly, was worth making. The Settlement involved careful work by theologians such as Thomas Cranmer, John Jewel and Richard Hooker. It required time. And constant vigilance.

Brexit and learning from the Reformation

Brexit has affected the UK like few other issues in recent memory. We have had to choose Remain or Leave, and we are split down the middle. Even our main political parties are unsure of how to handle things. Undoubtedly, the wounds of the past few years will take time to heal.

This is not to offer a view on Brexit. It is to suggest that if we are to learn anything from our history as a nation, it should be the dangers of allowing divisions to harden into irreconcilable hostility: we have been through civil war before. However, undertaking the kind of patient work that was required in the sixteenth and seventeenth centuries could bring our divided and polarized nation back together – although this will inevitably involve recognizing elements of value and truth in both the Remain and the Leave positions.

At the moment, this might seem an impossible task, given the scale of the divisions and the vehemence of the rhetoric. Taking a step back might offer a fresh perspective. Such a step might help us recognize that both sides of this debate are onto something. Both sides have a point.

The local and the universal

As I've suggested, our foray into sixteenth-century history, a seminal period in creating British identity, has something to say to us about Brexit. In the referendum of 2016, people voted one way or the other for all kinds of reasons. On the Leave side, the key issues were immigration, national sovereignty and the opportunity to forge new economic relationships across the world. The Remain argument tended to focus on international cooperation, the value of the EU in keeping European peace for seventy years, and the economic advantages of strong trading relationships with our nearest neighbours. You might say that, much as in the English Reformation, the debate was about the value of the local as opposed to the universal.

Every nation or ethnic group – even a unit as small as a city – has a history. Past events and dominant memories shape a body of people and, most importantly, give them a sense of identity. They will be aware of their own story, the language and sense of humour they share, the literature their ancestors have produced, the TV programmes they tend to watch, the values and commitments that make them who they are. If a society loses its particular cultural memory, people begin to feel rootless and life can appear shallow. They may find themselves lost in a modern, globalized world with no familiar landmarks to steer a path. As G. K. Chesterton once said, 'Nothing is real unless it is local.'

However, if all a society has is a strong and impregnable sense of its own identity, history and distinctiveness, it is in danger. Every society needs to be open to other cultures, to the history and insights of dissimilar people. Curiosity not only enlarges the imagination, but can act as a brake on a particular nation or state fossilizing, or developing a sense of cultural superiority over others. Ethnic pride can become dangerous – and we all know where it may lead.

The Leave vote was, at least in part, a cry of protest against what was perceived as a threat to national identity, whether through mass immigration, the vision of an increasingly federal Europe (that promised to erode national identity and sovereignty), or a globalization that threatened local culture. And it appeared as if there was a wealthy elite backing Leave, who had become divorced from the perspectives and hopes of a large swathe of people across the nation.[2] Some Leave voters felt they no longer recognized the country they lived in, and sensed its true identity and uniqueness were being eroded by rapid social change that had left them behind.[3] The argument about sovereignty was a cry to regain control and local responsibility. As one Leave voter put it, 'Our politicians may still make awful decisions, but at least they are accountable to us.'

The Remain vote, on the other hand, largely came from those who value openness to other cultures and desire to change and develop. They feared ethnic and national rigidity and favoured the possibilities and opportunities offered by engagement with our nearest neighbours. They were quite comfortable with the status quo and not overly worried about a loss of national identity: their horizons were larger and more international.

David Goodhart puts forward a similar argument in his book *The Road to Somewhere: The New Tribes Shaping British Politics*, published the year after the referendum.[4] He sees the new divide as not between left and right, but between 'somewheres' and 'anywheres'. 'Somewheres' are people with roots in a particular place, often a small town or the countryside. They may have deep and perhaps generational identification with this specific location and intense loyalty to it. He argues (although it is of course a generalization) that such people tend to be less well educated and cosmopolitan than 'anywheres'. Those who fall into this second grouping are often university educated (so likely to have moved away from home, family and childhood neighbourhoods), feel comfortable about social mobility and be less attached to a particular place. Goodhart estimates that 'somewheres' account for about half the population and 'anywheres' about 25 per cent. The remainder don't quite fit into either camp.

Goodhart's distinction maps well onto the local versus universal one I am drawing attention to here, yet my point is that both are necessary. Every healthy society needs a careful balance of these two impulses. A loss of identity and rootedness leads to a fading of cultural memory, a lack of belonging and a diminishing sense of who we are as a nation. Our history, language and ways of living differ from those of Germans, Brazilians, Americans or the French. We are shaped by the Anglo-Saxon conquest of Britain, the English Civil War, the Monarchy, the Church, Parliament, the Empire, the First and Second World Wars, our football teams, cricket, the contribution of generations of immigrants over the years, and so on. We have a sense of humour and ways of relating to one another that other nations notice perhaps more than we do – they are, after all, often the stuff of our jokes! We may like or dislike some of these factors, but they and many others have made Britain what it is, for better or for worse.

Yet what if we close ourselves off from other cultures, shut the door to neighbours (especially when they are in trouble), fail to play our part in wider conversations about the global future, and show reluctance to change? Such behaviour is dangerous. It can lead to the objectification of others, and a lack of compassion for those who are dissimilar to us. Like it or not, we have been shaped to some extent by our relationships with other countries, whether our nearest neighbours in Europe, the nations that used to be part of the British Empire, or those with whom we share a common language. The reality is that local cultural identity is constantly adapting to the influences of other people and other ways of living as newcomers settle in these islands and make their impact here – a process accelerated by globalization, the internet and social media.

Whether or not we like to admit it, and hard as it may be to acknowledge due to the heat generated by the arguments of the last few years, *both sides of the debate have a point*.

Every society needs to value what makes it distinct. We are born to particular parents, into a specific family and neighbourhood, at a certain time in history. These factors help shape and form each of us into a unique human being. Diversity in this sense is a good thing, both for individuals and for nations, for if we were all like one another, it would be deadly dull. At the same time, every society must be aware that it has blind spots, and that while its particular culture is to be celebrated, it has much to learn from the cultures of other groups who make up the human race. Alongside diversity, we need a sense of our underlying common bonds.

The problem with the referendum was that it forced us to choose between these two, and not surprisingly, roughly half of us came down on one side, and half came down on the other. It might help to imagine that it was a bit like asking Christians to decide whether Christ was human or divine, and forcing them to choose between the two options. They would find it impossible to answer because he is both! Of course, there are absolutely convinced Leavers and absolutely convinced Remainers, but many people report that it was very difficult to decide how to vote, and they opted for one way over the other only marginally. As one young woman put it: 'It was a really close decision and I wasn't 100 per cent sure that I wanted to leave because I could see pros and cons for both arguments.' The binary nature of the vote, and the way in which the debate has been conducted since, has tended to polarize even borderline voters into fanatics. When arguments get heated, it is very easy to become blind to the virtues of the other perspective.

In essence, the debate has been so painful and awkward because we have been forced to take sides on two impulses that we instinctively feel need to live in tension with each other.

Whatever the outcome, the task for the future is to move on from this unfortunate polarization. There will be those who argue fervently for the value of local communities, whose priority is to guard the things we depend on for our sense of identity and our understanding of Britain's place in the world. There will be those who continue to defend – just as fervently – the need for openness to, and curiosity about, the wider world, urging us to eschew the dangers of myopic narrowness. The job of those who lead us into the future will be to balance and harmonize these passions – whichever side of EU fence we happen to be, inside or outside.

We cannot afford to lose what makes Britain distinct and unique and quirkily itself. Neither can we pull up the drawbridge and become fortress Britain against the world, drifting into cultural superiority and racial pride. Our leaders need to get back to the age-old political task of harmonizing the past and the future, identity and openness, the local and the universal.

How can that be done? Is it just a pipe-dream?

How to love
your neighbour

The conundrum that Brexit sets us involves competing loves. How do I love my nearest and dearest, my family, those I identify with because they share my outlook on life, my values and my background – and those whose skin colour, political beliefs or circumstances may be different from mine?

One of the best-known parts of the teaching of Jesus, repeated often by the early Christians, is the call to 'love your neighbour as yourself'.[5] Here we see Jesus expanding on this, fully aware of the competing calls on our attention:

> You have heard that it was said, 'Love your neighbour and hate your enemy.' But I tell you, love your enemies and pray for those who persecute you, that you may be children of your Father in heaven. He causes his sun to rise on the evil and the good, and sends rain on the

righteous and the unrighteous. If you love those who love you, what reward will you get? Are not even the tax collectors doing that? And if you greet only your own people, what are you doing more than others? Do not even pagans do that? Be perfect, therefore, as your heavenly Father is perfect.

(Matthew 5.43–47)

It is possible to discern here four kinds of love. The first is love for ourselves. Before the call to love our neighbours, there is the assumption that most of us take care of ourselves, ensuring we have enough to eat and somewhere to sleep, that we look after our health and maintain friendships to sustain us, and so on. We have to assume responsibility for ourselves. We can't leave that to others by neglecting our health, welfare or prospects. Yet if taking care of ourselves is all we do, something is wrong. The person who is consumed by self-love, the narcissist who has no interest in anyone but themselves, is simply a pain in the neck. And that is because a second kind of love asks us to give the same attention we lavish on ourselves to those nearest to us, those tied to us by bonds of family and friendship, those whom Jesus calls 'those who love you'.

For most people, this is still fairly undemanding. Seeking the welfare of those who rely on us and those we have strong reasons to care for comes quite naturally. Yes, families can be difficult, but blood ties are strong and even in the toughest situations, it's hard to walk away. Friends or lovers are usually easier to love because we have chosen them ourselves! That's why Jesus can, in this teaching, assume that we tend to love 'those who love us'.

Yet even that doesn't go far enough. Jesus says: 'If you love those who love you, what reward will you get? Are not even the tax collectors doing that? And if you greet only your own people, what are you doing more than others?' In other words, if loving those who love you is relatively easy, the next stage is to learn to love your neighbour.

Your neighbour is the person you have no particular reason to love. They are not related to you; they are not a friend. They just happen to live next door, work at the desk next to yours, or stand at the same bus stop every morning. Søren Kierkegaard called love of neighbour the highest form of human love, because it is not what he termed 'preferential'. In other words, it is not based on some quality in the beloved that draws out your love. It is love that doesn't pick and choose – it simply loves the neighbour, the person next door, whoever they happen to be.[6]

Yet Jesus goes beyond even neighbour love to expect a fourth kind – love for our enemies: 'Love your enemies and pray for those who persecute you.' This is the perfection of love, being capable of loving not only yourself, not only those who love you, not only your neighbour, who happens to have strayed across your path but has no particular feeling toward you one way or the other – but the person who makes life hard for you, the one who really dislikes you, the one who is your rival, your foe. 'Be perfect therefore, as your heavenly father is perfect.' This is the kind of love that encourages the growth of a really healthy society, one where enmity is overcome and hurts healed.

As many texts in the Bible suggest, and Jesus liberally demonstrates, love in Christianity is not primarily a feeling. It is a set of actions. Loving your neighbour (or even your enemy) as yourself does not mean holding warm sentiments or attraction to them, or even liking them. It requires that you do for the other person what you would do for yourself. So if you take care of your own basic needs by ensuring you have enough to eat, safe shelter and somewhere to sleep, access to healthcare, leisure time to enjoy and contact with good friends, then loving your neighbour (or your enemy) demands you make sure – as far as you are able – that they have those things as well.

Loving your enemy feels a stretch. It demands much of us to love the person who is after our job, or changing our neighbourhood or nation into something unrecognizable, or taking the opposite view from us on everything – including Brexit.

That is where the relationship between the four loves comes in. Jesus' words suggest a kind of progression in love, a process of personal and spiritual growth. Love begins with the simplest form: self-love. The next lesson is to learn to love 'those who love us' with the same love we show ourselves. This will involve taking care of them, paying attention to their basic needs, ensuring, as much as we are able, that they thrive. Learning to love those who love us tends to begin in early childhood and continue as we grow; it is a stage in learning to love our neighbour. And learning to love our neighbour, who we haven't chosen, is an important step in the final stage of love – being able to reach out to love our enemy. As the French philosopher Simone Weil once wrote, 'Friendship . . . consists in loving a human being as we should love each soul in particular.'[7]

Despite what the Brexit debate has suggested, *these are not necessarily competing loves*. Love is not a limited commodity; it is not something we need to dole out sparingly. The more love takes root within us, the more it becomes part of our character, affecting our outlook and the way in which we respond to whomever crosses our path, whether family member, neighbour or even enemy. Love tends to grow the more it is practised.

The Brexit debate has pitted regard for a familiar culture and those with whom we share a similar background *against* a responsibility for the wider world – for immigrants, refugees and those from other cultures. Yet we do not *need* to choose between them. Of course, we shall be drawn more naturally to those who are like us, yet if we regard that 'natural' love not as selfishness (and certainly not as racism), but as the first stage in learning to love the stranger, then perhaps we can get somewhere. Similarly, if we regard concern for the immigrant, the refugee, the ethnically different not as a licence to neglect our immediate family and neighbours (and certainly not as a lack of patriotism), but as the growth of love for those who don't necessarily love us, then we may begin to build a coherent social life again.

If we love our neighbours and even our enemies, but not our friends or family, taking time for the immigrant without paying any attention to the needs of our immediate neighbours, the health of our local community and those most affected by social and economic change in our immediate communities, then something is seriously wrong. We have failed to learn the basics of love. Yet if we love our family but not our neighbours, our friends but not our enemies, then we remain spiritually adolescent, refusing to grow up.

In truth, the challenge the Brexit debate poses after the divisions of recent years is essentially not political, economic or legal but spiritual. Yes, there are political factors: we must seek to forge a new structure for our political life outside the European Union in light of the many questions asked about our democratic processes since the referendum. Yes, there are legal questions: the relationship between the judiciary and government has certainly come to the fore. Yes, there are economic questions: how shall we create new markets and new trading agreements with other parts of the world? Love for our neighbour needs to be fleshed out in a legal, political and economic system that fairly protects the identity of local communities, but enables us to learn from the wider world. That is not an easy task, given the fraught issues of immigration, international law and trade deals, yet the hard work must be done.

Remembering the effort made after the Reformation may inspire us to recognize the valid insights of both sides of the Brexit debate. Ultimately, the most important question is whether we can rise to the spiritual challenge of learning to love both friend and foe, family and neighbour, those who are like us and those who are not.

Conclusion

There are at least five things we badly need in the coming years to bring the nation back together:

1 *A commitment to the long haul*
The salutary tale of the English Reformation tells us that leaving the EU is just the beginning, not the end. After such a divisive debate and a bruising few years, it will take a long time to heal the divides and we must be alert to the dangers along the way.

2 *Recognizing the grain of truth in the position we oppose*
Brexit, like the English Reformation, is a moment in our history when we decided to take a radical step away from a centralizing European movement, and a step towards a new kind of independence, for better or for worse. The Reformation stands as both a warning and an invitation:

we have seen what can happen if division is allowed to harden into hatred and violence; yet we are invited to do the slow, patient work of recognizing the value in different opinions.

Now this is hard. The debate has been so painful that it may feel almost impossible to acknowledge that the other side has a point, especially when for some, Brexit might lead to the loss of something deeply valued and seem like a profound mistake – one that will affect generations to come. It can be equally difficult for the winning side, in the euphoria of victory, to appreciate the point that the opposition was trying to make. When all your efforts are focused on winning, you tend to be blind to other kinds of thinking. Yet attempts must be made on both sides. There is no other way.

3 *A commitment to truth-telling*
It was probably the Greek dramatist Aeschylus who originally said, 'In war, truth is the first casualty.' Truth also suffers in polarized, visceral political debate. As in

the Reformation period, we have seen today how very easy it is to slip into exaggeration, bias or downright lie to win an argument. Remainers could point to the £350m figure on the Brexit bus that supposedly went to the EU and might otherwise be spent on the NHS, or the fear that Turkey was soon to join the EU and that Britain would have no say. Leavers could point to what they called 'Project Fear' – the predictions of economic disaster that would result from Brexit. Truth matters, and it takes discipline to resist the temptation to twist figures and fabricate facts in order to boost one's own case. If we really are in a 'post-truth' era, then we shall find it very difficult to discern a wise way ahead. There is a danger we shall be swayed, not by reliable prediction and evidence, but by whoever can offer the most rhetorically alarming statistics. A commitment to telling the truth is vital.

4 *A renewal of local democracy*
Part of our problem is that our emphasis on national politics and personal consumerism has weakened the vitality

of local community life. Healing the disillusionment many people feel with national or pan-national politics will require a revival of the kind of local democracy that the parish system gave to communities in the past. Our challenge today is not to bring Catholic and Protestant together, but Leavers and Remainers. Local democracy would enable voices to be heard on the issues that matter to their community and allow for regional and local differences. Yet communities could be part of a wider pattern of national representation that would aim to prevent local differences from drifting into hostility or suspicion.

5 *A common story*

The post-Reformation Church of England was able to hold together due to belief in a common Christian story, even if that story was interpreted differently in different places. In other words, there was an attempt to create a new unity despite divisions. Without a common underlying set of beliefs and convictions, it will be hard to find any kind of unity for the nation going forward. That will be a challenge.

Yet it is not one we are without resources to meet. Jesus said God 'causes his sun to rise on the evil and the good, and sends rain on the righteous and the unrighteous'. At the core of the Christian faith is the conviction that every person, regardless of wealth, social status, gender or even moral goodness is equal as a recipient of God's love and attention. This argument is made powerfully by Tom Holland in his book *Dominion: The Making of the Western Mind*[8] when he speaks of the roots of human rights, the equality of persons and the value of the poor being found in the Christian faith that shaped Europe for centuries. In that vision, the purpose of human life was to become the kind of person capable of something as simple, yet mind-stretching as this: 'Love your enemies and pray for those who persecute you, that you may be children of your Father in heaven.'

Such a vision of society could give us a reason to learn to love not just ourselves and our nearest and dearest, but also our neighbours – in the same street or town, in Europe or beyond, whatever their colour or origin – and even our enemies. If we can do that, then we may just be able to bring the nation together beyond Brexit.

Notes

1 In one sense the argument continues. The recent commemoration of 500 years since the Reformation saw a number of books still arguing about this. Brad S. Gregory in *The Unintended Reformation: How a Religious Revolution Secularized Society* (Cambridge, Mass.: Belknap Press, Harvard, 2012) contended that the Reformation and the fracturing of a united European Christendom led to a corrosive, consumerist materialism and a loss of a common moral vision for society. Others, such as Alister McGrath in *Christianity's Dangerous Idea: The Protestant Revolution* (London: SPCK, 2007), argued that the Reformation movement was an essential revolution leading to such vital notions as freedom of conscience and religion, human rights, universal education, and so on.

2 This perspective is given eloquent voice in works such as Douglas Murray in *The Strange Death of Europe: Immigration, Identity, Islam* (Bloomsbury, London: 2017).

3 Danny Dorling, Professor of Geography at Oxford University, has suggested that the Leave vote came not from the working classes in industrial northern towns, as is a common myth, but from a disenchanted 'middle England' (citing that 59 per cent of the Leave

vote came from middle class people) and older people feeling the effects of a declining NHS and increasing inequality across the nation.

4 David Goodhart, *The Road to Somewhere: The New Tribes Shaping British Politics* (Penguin, London: 2017).

5 Matthew 22.39; Mark 12.31; Luke 10.27; Romans 13.9; Galatians 5.14.

6 Søren Kierkegaard, *Works of Love* (Harper Perennial, New York: 1962).

7 Simone Weil, *Waiting for God* (HarperCollins, New York: 2009).

8 Tom Holland, *Dominion: The Making of the Western Mind* (Little Brown, London: 2019).

Bibliography

Goodhart, D. *The Road to Somewhere: The New Tribes Shaping British Politics* (London: Penguin, 2017).

Gregory, B. S. *The Unintended Reformation: How a Religious Revolution Secularized Society* (Cambridge, Mass.: Belknap Press, Harvard, 2012).

Holland, T. *Dominion: The Making of the Western Mind* (London: Little Brown, 2019).

Kierkegaard, S. *Works of Love* (Harper Perennial, New York: 1962).

McGrath, A. *Christianity's Dangerous Idea: The Protestant Revolution* (London: SPCK, 2007).

Murray, D. *The Strange Death of Europe: Immigration, Identity, Islam* (London: Bloomsbury, 2017).

Weil, S. *Waiting for God* (HarperCollins, New York: 2009).

This reflection will appear in

THE FUTURE OF BREXIT BRITAIN

Anglican Reflections on National Identity
and European Solidarity

Edited by

Jonathan Chaplin and Andrew Bradstock

15 October 2020 • £12.99

Pre-order at a special discounted price

from SPCK Publishing

www.spckpublishing.co.uk